THE MYSTERY OF THE MARY CELESTE

by Barbara Krasner

Content Consultant
James C. Bradford
Department of History
Texas A&M University

Core Library

An Imprint of Abdo Publishing
abdopublishing.com

abdopublishing.com

Published by Abdo Publishing, a division of ABDO, PO Box 398166, Minneapolis, Minnesota 55439. Copyright © 2016 by Abdo Consulting Group, Inc. International copyrights reserved in all countries. No part of this book may be reproduced in any form without written permission from the publisher. Core Library™ is a trademark and logo of Abdo Publishing.

Printed in the United States of America, North Mankato, Minnesota
082015
012016

THIS BOOK CONTAINS
RECYCLED MATERIALS

Cover Photo: DeAgostini/Getty Images
Interior Photos: DeAgostini/Getty Images, 1; Wikimedia Commons, 4, 17, 43; Hulton Archive/
Getty Images, 7, 18, 45; Mary Evans Picture Library/Alamy, 8, 14, 25, 30; Red Line Editorial, 11;
Shutterstock Images, 13; DeAgostini Picture Library/Getty Images, 20; AP Images, 22; adoc-
photos/Corbis, 28; Nick Ut/AP Images, 36; Ralph Bruce/Private Collection/Bridgeman Art, 39

Editor: Mirella Miller
Series Designer: Ryan Gale

Library of Congress Control Number: 2015945991

Cataloging-in-Publication Data
Krasner, Barbara.
 The mystery of the Mary Celeste / Barbara Krasner.
  p. cm. -- (Mysteries of history)
 ISBN 978-1-68078-024-6 (lib. bdg.)
 Includes bibliographical references and index.
 1. Mary Celeste (Brig)--Juvenile literature.   I. Title.
 910--dc23

                                                    2015945991

CONTENTS

CHAPTER ONE

A DESERTED SHIP ADRIFT

No one knows who first sighted the two-masted ship on the Atlantic Ocean, 400 miles (644 km) from the Portuguese islands of the Azores. On December 5, 1872, aboard the British ship *Dei Gratia*, either Captain David Morehouse or seaman John Johnson spotted the sails of a ship 4 to 5 miles (6 to 8 km) away. The distant ship moved unsteadily and appeared to be in trouble. Despite high seas from

The Mary Celeste has been surrounded by mystery since it was found abandoned in 1872.

previous storms, Captain Morehouse brought his own ship closer and yelled to ask if it needed assistance. Captain Morehouse received no response. He did not see anyone either. This was not a good sign. He ordered Johnson, along with two other sailors, Oliver Deveau and John Wright, to take a small boat over to the ship. As they got closer, they could see the name of the vessel: *Mary Celeste*.

The Ghost Ship

Deveau and Wright climbed aboard the *Mary Celeste*. Deveau immediately set out to inspect the ship. The first step was to determine how much water was in the hold. There was nearly 3.5 feet (1.1 m) of water, which was too much. Deveau next inspected the pumps, which proved to be in good order. The men found no lifeboats, although they could see where one could have been. There were six months' worth of supplies in the storeroom and plenty of drinking water. There were also 1,700 barrels of alcohol. The compass stand and the compass were damaged. But

Captain Morehouse ordered some of his men to go and check on the abandoned ship.

the wheel was unharmed, and the topmast sail was set. Two of the sails had blown away, and another sail hung loose. Some of the rigging was also gone.

The sailors continued their search of the ship. They could not find the captain's measurement tools or the navigation book. They found the logbook on the captain's desk and a chalkboard on a cabin table. There were regular entries up until November 25, 1872. It read, "At 8 Eastern point bore S.S.W. 6 miles distant," indicating that the ship was 6 miles (10 km)

The Dei Gratia crew found food left on a table aboard the Mary Celeste.

east of the last Azores island. The line for 9:00 a.m. was blank.

The cabin was wet. The captain's bed was not made up, and Deveau could see the impression of a child in the bed. It seemed all the captain's furniture and clothing were just as he had left them. Deveau believed there must have been a woman on board too.

Deveau and Wright spent 30 minutes searching the ship. To Deveau, it seemed the captain and crew left in a hurry. But the ship

Dangerous Water, Dangerous Cargo

The autumn season often brought harsh weather and hazardous conditions to sailors. Fierce winds blowing at more than 60 miles per hour (97 km/h) and lasting a few days were common. The *Mary Celeste* logbook reported choppy seas and high winds for the last day or two before its final entry. Professional sailors knew the risks of sailing during autumn. But when hauling cargo such as alcohol or other flammable substances, that risk grew even greater and could threaten the lives of those aboard. Alcohol could easily be set on fire and explode.

appeared seaworthy. The masts were good and the ship even appeared somewhat new. They found no one aboard. The ship had clearly been abandoned. Deveau, Wright, and Johnson returned to the *Dei Gratia* and reported their findings to Captain Morehouse.

With reward money in mind, Deveau asked Captain Morehouse's permission to take two men and sail the abandoned ship to Gibraltar, a British naval base at the entrance to the Mediterranean Sea 600 miles (966 km) away.

The *Mary Celeste* Sails to Gibraltar

Morehouse considered Deveau's proposal and the risk involved. These were dangerous waters, and both the *Dei Gratia* and the *Mary Celeste* were small ships. Morehouse had his own mission to complete. He was hauling petroleum but did not yet know his final destination. He would get further instructions at Gibraltar.

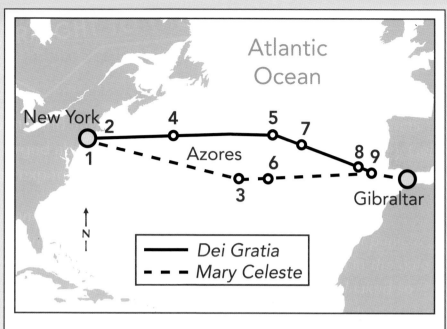

1. *Mary Celeste* sailed from New York on November 7
2. *Dei Gratia* sailed from New York on November 15
3. November 14
4. November 19
5. December 1
6. November 25: 8:00 a.m.
7. December 2
8. December 5: Noon
9. December 5: 1:00 p.m.
   Mary Celeste and *Dei Gratia* meet at this point

Route of the *Mary Celeste* and the *Dei Gratia*

Ship captains kept detailed records of their ships' positions, citing longitude and latitude. What can you learn about the *Mary Celeste* from this map? The last logbook entry appeared on November 25. What does this map show about the *Mary Celeste*'s route before the *Dei Gratia* discovered it on December 5?

Morehouse could not ignore the reward money he could make from bringing in an abandoned ship. Then there was the cargo itself. The 1,700 barrels of alcohol could bring in a lot of money. Morehouse agreed to Deveau's proposal. He assigned two other sailors to Deveau and allowed them to use the small boat, a barometer, a compass, and a watch.

The *Dei Gratia* arrived at the port of Gibraltar the evening of December 12. The *Mary Celeste*, under Deveau's

Modern day Gibraltar from the top of the city's mountains

command, arrived at Gibraltar early in the morning on December 13. Its crew was exhausted. They had hit a storm. Wanting to rest, Deveau was not prepared for what came next. The *Mary Celeste* was immediately placed under arrest.

CHAPTER TWO

ANOTHER VOYAGE

Captain Benjamin Spooner Briggs grew up in a family of New England sailors. His father and four brothers all became ship captains. Briggs was 38 years old when he took command of the *Mary Celeste*. He was an experienced and well-respected officer.

On October 19, 1872, Briggs traveled from his Marion, Massachusetts, home to New York. There

The *Mary Celeste*'s trip to Italy should have been a relatively safe one.

A Seafaring Family

Benjamin Briggs came from a family of sailors. He lost two brothers to yellow fever while aboard ships. Another brother was lost at sea. His only sister drowned on her husband's ship. His father Captain Nathan Briggs died from a lightning strike while standing in his doorway. Some believed the Briggs family was as doomed as the *Mary Celeste*. But Benjamin Briggs knew living at sea held its own misfortunes.

he would prepare for his voyage to Genoa, Italy. His wife, Sarah, and their two-year-old daughter, Sophia Matilda, arrived in New York one week later. Briggs's seven-year-old son, Arthur, had just started school. He stayed behind with his grandmother so he could keep up with his lessons.

The *Mary Celeste* loaded its cargo hold with barrels of industrial alcohol. Food and water were brought on board. Captain Briggs had a crew of seven men. Each man had specific tasks to perform on the ship to help it run properly. Sarah had a small piano brought on board. The ship would be filled with music.

Captain Benjamin Briggs

New York's waterfront was crowded with ships and the men who commanded them. Captain Briggs hoped to find one of his brothers among them. They were all seamen and did not see each other often. Instead, he ran into Captain Morehouse of the *Dei*

It is likely the piano Sarah brought on board the ship was used to entertain her husband and his crew.

Gratia. This ship would sail eight days after the *Mary Celeste*. According to some accounts, Morehouse had dinner with Briggs and Sarah.

Headed toward the Open Sea

The *Mary Celeste* was ready for its voyage to Italy. Briggs was proud of the ship. He owned one-third of it. He was not going to take any unnecessary risks. The ship had a shaky history. Some might have even said the ship was cursed. The *Mary Celeste* was built in 1861 in Nova Scotia, Canada, of local birch, maple, and beech wood. It was given the name the *Amazon*.

It had trouble from the start. Its first captain died. It then ran aground during fierce winds in 1867. Poorly maintained, it was sold and refitted in New York. Now an American ship, it was renamed the *Mary Celeste* in 1868. By 1872 it was sold again to Briggs and two other investors.

The ship pulled up anchor as planned on November 5. As it headed toward the open sea, a storm was brewing. Captain Briggs made a decision. He thought it best to stay close to the harbor until the weather cleared. Could this false start have been an omen

PERSPECTIVES
Can a Ship Be Cursed?

When bad things continuously happened to a ship and its passengers, people began to believe the ship was cursed. Sailors in the 1800s often told tales of finding abandoned ships. They also told stories of ships that were doomed from the time they first set sail. Can a ship really be cursed? Could a storm on the day of setting sail be a sign of future bad luck? Modern scientific methods and logic can explain weather conditions, illness, poor maintenance, and other factors that created the myths of cursed ships.

Captain Morehouse and his crew noticed some of the sails were ripped on the *Mary Celeste*, a sign weather was a factor in the abandonment of the ship's crew.

of bad things to come? Two days later, the *Mary Celeste* weighed anchor again and sailed into the open sea. The people on board would never be seen again, alive or dead.

Captain Briggs's wife, Sarah, wrote a letter to her mother-in-law in Massachusetts after a false start toward the open sea:

Dear Mother Briggs—

Probably you will be a little surprised to receive a letter with this date, but instead of proceeding out to sea when we came out Tuesday morning, we anchored about a mile or so from the city, as it was strong head wind, and B. [Captain Benjamin Briggs] said it looked so thick & nasty ahead . . . Accordingly we took a fresh departure this morning.

Source: Charles Edey Fay. The Story of the "Mary Celeste." New York: Dover Publications, 1988. Print. 11.

What's the Big Idea?

Read the text carefully. What is its main idea? How do details support the main idea? Name three of them.

AN INVESTIGATION, BUT NO REAL ANSWERS

On December 18, five days after Deveau brought the *Mary Celeste* to Gibraltar, an investigation began. The ship had been taken into custody because Captain Morehouse had put in a claim, along with the *Dei Gratia* crew and its owners, for the reward money from the *Mary Celeste*. The investigation meant there would be a hearing. The court would determine whether the men should

As with any abandoned ship found at sea during the 1800s, an investigation needed to be conducted on the *Mary Celeste*.

receive the money and how much they would earn. This procedure was routine for abandoned ships.

On December 18, the chief justice of the court, Sir James Cochrane, began the hearing. Frederick Solly-Flood, the advocate general of the court, represented the government. Henry Pisani represented the interests of the *Dei Gratia* captain and crew, while George Cornwell represented the owners of the *Mary Celeste*. His job was to show the *Mary Celeste* had not been abandoned and should be returned to the remaining owners without paying a reward to Morehouse and his men. Pisani had to prove his clients had rightful claim to the salvage money.

Witnesses Take the Stand

The court first called on Deveau to give his account of what happened when they found the *Mary Celeste*. His testimony and all those that followed were recorded. Deveau talked about sighting the *Mary Celeste*. He described what he found when he went

During the trial, Deveau walked the court through each step he and the other *Dei Gratia* crew members had taken.

on board. He explained how he found the logbook and the chalkboard on the cabin table.

Deveau also noted the *Dei Gratia* met stormy weather from November 15 to November 24. One could only guess the *Mary Celeste* had experienced the same conditions. He could see where a lifeboat might have been. But there was no proof that there had been one.

Deveau revealed more details through Cochrane's and Solly-Flood's questioning. The logbook was presented as evidence. So was the chalkboard. The judge scheduled the next session for two days later on December 20.

On December 20, Deveau took the stand again. He talked about finding a woman's clothes. He described

Tampering with Evidence

In an investigation, evidence is presented to the court. Evidence can help to prove or disprove a case. In the case of the *Mary Celeste*, the crew of the *Dei Gratia* did not find most of the ship's tools aboard. However, Deveau found the logbook and the chalkboard. According to his own testimony, Deveau unintentionally rubbed off the writing on the board. In its place he made his own entries. This could be considered destroying the evidence. Could the mystery of the *Mary Celeste* have been solved if that information was not gone?

seeing where a small child might have slept on a bed. Deveau also described a small piano in the cabin. Charts showing the *Mary Celeste*'s route were presented as evidence.

Now it was Wright's turn to tell his side of the story. It agreed with Deveau's account. The other sailors made their statements on December 20 and 21. James Henry Winchester, who owned half the *Mary Celeste*, arrived in Gibraltar to give his testimony in January 1873. The court met again on January 29. Captain Morehouse gave his account on March 3.

PERSPECTIVES
The Search for Survivors

According to one account, years after both Morehouse and Deveau died, Morehouse's widow told a Boston reporter about her husband's friendship with Captain Briggs. Morehouse knew the *Mary Celeste* was Briggs's ship. Mrs. Morehouse suggested her husband conducted a desperate yet unsuccessful search for Briggs, his passengers, and crew. However, journalists and historians continue to debate his actions.

Bad weather and storms are a possible reason for the *Mary Celeste* being abandoned.

The *Mary Celeste* Undergoes Examination

Solly-Flood found it difficult to believe these witnesses. If the ship was found in good working order, what happened to the people? He ordered an examination of the *Mary Celeste*. Even though this survey of the ship lasted several hours, Solly-Flood was not satisfied. He ordered another survey. The ship proved seaworthy. It showed no evidence of bad weather or an explosion. After his examination, the Gibraltar Surveyor of Shipping certified that only one of the pumps was found to be in good working order. The other pump's valve was removed. One object continued to hold Solly-Flood's attention. It was a sword with what he believed were traces of blood. The abandonment of the *Mary Celeste* was a mystery. But Solly-Flood had his own theories about the truth.

FURTHER EVIDENCE

Chapter Three talks about the investigation into the *Mary Celeste*'s abandonment. Watch the short video at the link below. Can you find information from the video that supports the author's point? Write a few sentences using information from the video as evidence to support the main point of this chapter.

The *Mary Celeste*
mycorelibrary.com/mary-celeste

CHAPTER FOUR

MYSTERY SHROUDS THE SHIP

There were many opinions about what actually happened to the *Mary Celeste*. Pirates could have overtaken the ship. Or perhaps the crew overtook the ship. Maybe a terrible storm caused the ship to drift. Some believed Captain Briggs went mad. Someone could have killed the captain and his family. Maybe Captain Briggs and Captain Morehouse developed a scheme to make it seem like the ship was

There are many theories as to why the crew could have abandoned the ship and jumped overboard.

Sir Arthur Conan Doyle Creates a Myth

Were it not for Sir Arthur Conan Doyle, the *Mary Celeste* might have slipped into history. In 1884 this creator of the Sherlock Holmes detective stories wrote a short story, "J. Habakuk Jephson's Statement." He changed the name of the ship to the *Marie Celeste*. He wrote an account convincingly from the point of view of a passenger aboard the ship. Readers believed the story to be true. Doyle's story created even more mystery about the ship. In his version, a passenger creates trouble for everyone on board. He kills the captain and his family. After Doyle's story, would anyone learn the truth about the *Mary Celeste*?

abandoned so they could collect the money. It could have been that the crew was afraid the alcohol on board would cause an explosion.

Solly-Flood, though, suspected foul play. An independent analysis of wood from the *Mary Celeste*'s deck and cabin floor as well as the sword concluded there was no blood to be found. Cochrane also suspected foul play. He thought there was something not quite right about the behavior of the *Dei Gratia* crew. Morehouse and his crew suffered from continued suspicion the rest of their lives.

Rejected Theories

With further investigations and surveys, many theories were rejected. Rebellion was ruled out. All theories aside, what was known is that something disturbing happened on the *Mary Celeste* after November 25 at 8:00 a.m. There was a great hurry. Perhaps the captain and crew on the lifeboat hoped they would be back on the ship very soon.

PERSPECTIVES
A Ship with a Reputation

The *Mary Celeste* earned a reputation as a ghost ship. No one wanted to work on it or hire it. It passed through several owners. In 1885 its last commander, Captain Gilman C. Parker, decided to run the ship aground on a Haitian reef for the insurance money. Parker was arrested and died three months later. All companies involved with the ship went bankrupt. Until the very end, the *Mary Celeste* appeared to bring bad luck to anyone associated with it.

After hearing three months' worth of testimonies and examining evidence from the *Mary Celeste*, some theories, such as murder or piracy, appeared unreasonable. Others, such as a threat of alcohol fumes and possible explosion, seemed more reasonable. The hearing ended in March 1873. The owners and the *Dei Gratia* crew received money, but not the full value. The *Mary Celeste* was finally released to its surviving owners. The ship could now continue on to its original destination of Genoa.

EXPLORE ONLINE

This chapter discusses the various theories about why no people were found aboard the *Mary Celeste*. Explore the video on the website below. Compare and contrast the information found in the video with that found in this chapter. What differences do you notice? What similarities can you find?

The True Story of the *Mary Celeste*

mycorelibrary.com/mary-celeste

During and after the Gibraltar court inquiry, many theories emerged about why no one was found aboard the *Mary Celeste*. One expert was asked to examine the ship and offer his opinion:

> *I am of the opinion that she [the Mary Celeste] was abandoned by the master & crew in a moment of panic & for no sufficient reason. She may have strained in the gale through which she was passing & for the time leaked so much as to alarm the Master, and it is possible that, at this moment, another vessel in sight, induced him (having his wife and child on board,) to abandon thus hastily.*
>
> Source: Charles Edey Fay. The Story of the 'Mary Celeste.' New York: Dover Publications, 1988. Print. 86.

Changing Minds

This text passage gives one explanation for Captain Briggs to abandon ship. Take his position and then imagine your best friend disagrees and has the opposite opinion. Write a short essay trying to change your friend's mind. Make sure you detail your opinion and your reasons for it. Include facts and details that support your reasons.

CHAPTER FIVE

NEW MILLENNIUM, NEW QUESTIONS

The *Mary Celeste* rested in its watery grave in Haiti until 2001. Then author and marine archaeologist Clive Cussler, long fascinated by the tale of this ship, wanted to find its remains. At first he and his crew met many problems. Their boat's propeller was damaged. They faced stormy conditions. Was the curse of the *Mary Celeste* still alive?

Clive Cussler hoped his research would find the remains of the *Mary Celeste* and solve the mystery of its abandonment.

They traveled to Rochelais Reef where they believed the *Mary Celeste* had sunk. Divers found fragments of wood, iron, and copper near the reef. This was hardly a reef now. Instead, it was millions of conch shells. Cussler and his crew sent samples of their findings to scientists. The scientists verified the age and nature of the samples. They concluded Cussler had indeed found the *Mary Celeste*. Still, the mystery remained. Why had the captain, his family, and the crew left the ship?

PERSPECTIVES

Hunting Shipwrecks

Some people make their living by searching for the remains of shipwrecks. Some look for lost treasures. Others donate their findings to museums or to laboratories for scientific research. Still others sell their discoveries for large amounts of money. Hunting for shipwrecks requires experienced divers and archaeologists to survey and map the oceans. It may also need advanced technology, such as robots, to explore deep ocean depths.

Abandoned Ship Manned by Ghost Crew
This image shows the *Dei Gratia*'s sighting of the ghostly *Mary Celeste*. What do you notice about the two ships and the crew? How does the illustration help you understand the *Dei Gratia*'s reaction to sighting the *Mary Celeste*?

New Evidence Appears

Documentary filmmaker Anne MacGregor loved mysteries. She wanted to revisit the *Mary Celeste* and use technology available in the 2000s. She launched her own investigation. She used advanced technology to determine what could or could not have happened to the *Mary Celeste*. MacGregor examined

Solly-Flood's notes. Since the ship's log disappeared in 1885, Solly-Flood's notes provided the only record MacGregor could use to plot the course of the ship. She concluded the ship was actually 120 miles (193 km) west of where Captain Briggs thought he was. Briggs should have seen land three days before he did. Solly-Flood wrote that in the last five days of the *Mary Celeste*'s voyage, Briggs had changed course and headed north, perhaps to seek safety.

MacGregor's team also discovered the *Mary Celeste* had previously carried coal. Coal could have plugged the ship's pumps. This may be why Deveau found one pump taken apart. Without being able to see how much water was in the hold, Briggs could have ordered everyone to abandon ship. Any number of conditions could have made it difficult for Briggs and his crew to measure the water accurately.

No Definite Answers

Others still suggest the alcohol fumes on board were the culprit. The fumes threatened the ship.

The captain issued orders to abandon ship to let the *Mary Celeste* air out. It was a safety measure, in case the alcohol exploded. Once everyone was in the tiny lifeboat, the theory goes, the towline snapped, casting the lifeboat adrift.

Even with the use of modern technology, the fate of Captain Briggs, his family, and the crew remains a mystery. No one knows for sure what really happened on the *Mary Celeste*.

Ghost Ships

Some people claim the *Mary Celeste* was a ghost ship, but its remains were found. There were ships, however, that appeared out of nowhere to sailors. One such ghost ship known as the *Flying Dutchman* first appeared in writings in 1795 and has been talked about, and even sighted, years after. Legend has it the ship disappeared while rounding the Cape of Good Hope in South Africa. Another lost ship is the HMS *Eurydice*, a training vessel for the British navy. In 1878 it met up with an unexpected snowstorm and sank. The ship had two survivors. Still, there have been reports of ghostly sightings.

Unknown threats caused the crew to abandon ship.

Evidence for:

- No one was found aboard.
- The ship seemed to be sailing itself.

Evidence against:

- Modern technology can only suggest what caused the captain and crew to abandon ship.

Bad weather threw the *Mary Celeste* crew overboard or caused them to abandon ship.

Evidence for:

- The *Dei Gratia* had experienced bad weather from November 15 to November 24.
- Two sails had blown away and another hung loose.

Evidence against:

- The boat was in working condition.
- No notes were left about poor weather conditions.

The alcohol on board posed a real threat.

Evidence for:

- Nine of the 1,700 barrels had been opened.
- The industrial alcohol was most likely flammable.

Evidence against:

- Deveau found all barrels in safe condition.
- The leakage had only been found upon its arrival in Genoa, after the Gibraltar hearing.

STOP AND THINK

Take a Stand

Chapter Four talks about some of the theories connected with the disappearing crew of the *Mary Celeste*. Some suspected foul play by either the *Mary Celeste* or the *Dei Gratia* crew. Others believed pirates or the weather played a role. What do you think? Do the investigations affect your position? Why or why not?

You Are There

Chapter One describes how the *Dei Gratia* found the *Mary Celeste*. Imagine you were aboard the *Dei Gratia* at the time and Captain Morehouse requested you to check out the drifting ship. What thoughts would go through your mind as you step into the small ship? What do you think it feels like to examine a ship that has been abandoned? Write a letter to your friends telling them what it is like. Be sure to add plenty of detail to your notes.

Tell the Tale

Chapter Three discusses the court hearings in Gibraltar about the *Mary Celeste.* Imagine you are in the courtroom. Write 200 words about what you hear from the *Dei Gratia* crew, Frederick Solly-Flood, and Judge Cochrane. Is there anything you do not quite believe? Do you learn new facts about the abandoned ship?

Dig Deeper

After reading this book, what questions do you still have about the *Mary Celeste*? With an adult's help, find a few reliable sources that can help answer your questions. Write a paragraph about what you learned.

GLOSSARY

bankrupt
not having enough money to sufficiently operate a business or company

conch shells
seashells shaped like a horn

hold
the cargo deck of a ship

latitude
the distance, north or south, from Earth's equator

longitude
the distance east or west

rigging
the chains and ropes used to work and support the masts and sails

seaman
a sailor

testimony
an oral account given by a witness in a court trial or hearing

topmast
a mast above the lower mast that supports the topsails

LEARN MORE

Books

Matthews, Rupert. *Unexplained Disappearances.* Irvine, CA: QED Publishing, 2010.

Rice, Dona Herweck. *Unsolved! History's Mysteries.* Huntington Beach, CA: Teacher Created Materials, 2012.

Simon, Seymour. *Strange Mysteries from Around the World.* Mineola, NY: Dover, 2012.

Websites

To learn more about Mysteries of History, visit **booklinks.abdopublishing.com**. These links are routinely monitored and updated to provide the most current information available.

Visit **mycorelibrary.com** for free additional tools for teachers and students.

INDEX

ABOUT THE AUTHOR

Barbara Krasner is a children's book author who enjoys writing about US and world history. She lives in New Jersey and teaches writing at a local university.